I Can Celebrate the Jewish Holidays

by Joel Lurie Grishaver

Illustrated by David Bleicher

Design by Jane Golub

Torah Aura Productions

ISBN 10: 1-934527-33-5

ISBN 13: 978-1-934527-33-7

Illustraton © 2010 David Bleicher.

Photo/Illustration: Noam Armonn, page 34; Leland Bobbé, page 20; Odelia Cohen, page 61; Chaim Danziger 33, 39; Caroline DeVita 25; Enrico Fianchini 34; Fotalia I 28; Bonnie Gordon-Lucas 32; David Grossman/Alamy, page 68; Vladislav Gurfinkel, page 63; GW Images, page 14; Ella Hanochi, page 89; Imagesource, page 19; Holly Jones, page 55; Sean Locke, page 50; Roni Markowitz, page 56; Carmen Martinez Banus, page 94; Moti Meiri, pages 13, 87; Mordechai Meiri, pages 41, 47, 85; Christine B. Miller, page 86; Monkey Business, page 34; Paul B. Moore, page 17; Mtrommer, page 83; Ethan Myerson, page 34; Nextrecord, page 71; Noam, page 54; Raigordski Pavel, page 40; Michaela Pschorr, page 21; Carlos Restrepo, page 57; Reuters/CORBIS, page 84; Abba Richman, page 27; Pavlina Richterova, page 48; John Said, page 90; Jose Ignacio Soto, page 38; Andrey Sukhachev, page 18; Johan Swanepoel, page 11; Tova Teitelbaum, pages 50, 51; Cristine Tripp, page 54; Nathan Winter, page 38; Lisa F. Young, page 38; Victor Zastol'skiy, page 79.

Thank you to Seeka—Jewelry and Judaica (top) and Emily Rosenfeld (bottom) for use of the tzedakah boxes on page 37.

Torah Aura Productions • 4423 Fruitland Avenue, Los Angeles, CA 90058
(800) BE-Torah • (800) 238-6724 • (323) 585-7312 • fax (323) 585-0327
E-MAIL <misrad@torahaura.com> • Visit the Torah Aura website at www.torahaura.com

MANUFACTURED IN MALAYSIA

Table of Contents

3

The Jewish Year

The Jewish year is like a circle.
Every holiday tells a story.
Every year these stories
become a part of our
lives.

THE JEWISH YEAR

ROSH HA-SHANAH

YOM KIPPUR

SUKKOT

SIMHAT TORAH

SHABBAT

HANUKKAH

TU B'SHVAT

PURIM

PASSOVER

YOM HA-ATZMA'UT

SHAVUOT

ראש הַשָּׁנָה

Rosh
ha-Shanah

A New Year

Think about the first day of school.

The first day of school is both exciting and scary. It is a day when you worry about lots of questions.

Will this be a good year?

Will I make new friends?

Will my teacher like me?

Will I do well?

The first day of school is also a day for making wishes.

"I hope I have a good year."

"I hope everyone likes me."

"I hope I can be a good student."

Awe

The feeling of being both excited and scared at the same times is called awe. People feel awe when they meet someone famous. They feel it when they see a beautiful sunset. Something that is very exciting can also be very scary.

Rosh ha-Shanah means "Head of the Year." It comes about the same time as the start of school. It is a day for asking questions and making wishes.

Rosh ha-Shanah Customs

Rosh ha-Shanah is a time when we send cards to our friends and family. We send the wish *L'Shanah Tovah*—for a good year. Every Rosh ha-Shanah card is a hope for the best possible New Year.

Rosh ha-Shanah gives us a frest start. We leave last year behind and start again to be the best people we can become.

Jews prepare for Rosh ha-Shanah in many different ways.

Practicing blowing the shofar

Giving Tzedakah

Studying the mahzor

Sending
Rosh ha-Shanah cards

Saying "I'm sorry"

Remembering family history

One way I can get ready for Rosh ha-Shanah is _____

_____

_____

On Rosh ha-Shanah we eat apples and honey. We have a round _hallah_. We dip the <u>h</u>allah in honey. These are ways of wishing that the New Year will be sweet and good.

Rosh ha-Shanah is called The Birthday of the Universe. It isn't a day for parties. Rosh ha-Shanah is a time we set aside for thinking. We pray. We hope to be awakened by the call of the shofar.

Circle the things you do at a birthday party.

The items that are not circled are all part of Rosh ha-Shanah.

The Shofar

When we are asleep an alarm clock wakes us up.

On Rosh ha-Shanah the shofar is our alarm clock. It asks our hearts to become fully awake. It calls on each of us to pay attention to start the New Year.

This is a *shofar*. It is a ram's horn. It makes a loud sound. It is a sound that makes you pay attention. On Rosh ha-Shanah it is a mitzvah to hear to the shofar. The shofar teaches us how to begin the New Year.

The shofar makes three different sounds. Try making these sounds with your voice.

Teki'ah is one long loud blast.
It sounds like a person shouting.

Shevarim is three short blasts.
It sounds like a person groaning.

Teru'ah is nine quick blasts.
It sounds like a person crying.

The cantor calls out the names of the shofar blasts.

Teki'ah Shevarim Teru'ah Teki'ah
Teki'ah Shevarim Teki'ah
Teki'ah Teru'ah Teki'ah Gedolah.

The Maḥzor

In the synagogue we use a special prayer book called a *Maḥzor* on Rosh ha-Shanah.

Tashliḥ

On the first day of Rosh ha-Shanah many Jews go to the edge of a lake, river or ocean and throw pieces of bread into the water. This is a ceremony called *tashliḥ*. The bread stands for our sins. On Rosh ha-Shanah we are trying to throw our sins away.

Yom Kippur

This is a bathtub. It is a place where we wash off dirt and become clean again.

Atonement

Look at the word atonement.

Can you see two words hiding in it? Look carefully and you will find the words AT and ONE.

Yom Kippur is a day when we try to become clean in a different way. It is a day on which Jews wash away all the mistakes and bad things we have done in the past year. Yom Kippur is a day on which we return to being AT ONE with God.

Yom Kippur comes ten days after Rosh ha-Shanah.

Missing the Mark

The Rabbis used a bow and arrow to explain Yom Kippur. Even if you were the best archer in the world, sometimes you wouldn't hit the bull's-eye. Every once in a while your arrow would miss the mark.

Trying to be a good Jew is a lot like being an archer.

We want to be kind.

We want to control our tempers.

We never want to hurt anyone.

Even when we try with all our might, we sometimes miss the mark.

Al Het

On Yom Kippur we have an opportunity to think about the things we have done that missed the mark. We say a prayer called *Al Het* that reminds us of the times we missed the mark and helps us to think about how we will do better next year.

Put a check next to the correct answers.

1. In the past year, I have missed the mark by using words to hurt others.

   ☐ Not at all ☐ A little
   ☐ Some ☐ A lot

2. In the past year, I have missed the mark by lying.

   ☐ Not at all ☐ A little
   ☐ Some ☐ A lot

3. In the past year, I have missed the mark by not respecting my parents and teachers.

   ☐ Not at all ☐ A little
   ☐ Some ☐ A lot

T'shuvah

On Yom Kippur we use thoughts, songs and prayers to make our hearts clean again. This is doing *t'shuvah*. *T'shuvah* lets you fix something that hurt another person and say "I will never do that again."

God will forgive us if we really do *t'shuvah* on Yom Kippur. But we must first ask anyone we have hurt for forgiveness.

19

What We Do on Yom Kippur

Yom Kippur starts at night. One of the first prayers we say is called *Kol Nidre*. Everyone stands. The Torah scrolls are taken out of the ark.

Kol Nidre means "all my vows." It asks God to forgive us for all the promises made last year that we couldn't keep.

By fasting and spending a whole day in prayer, we use all our strength to fix the things we have done that missed the mark. We try to do *t'shuvah* with all our hearts. The words in the *mahzor* explain our hopes that on Yom Kippur we can atone and return to being AT ONE with God.

Sukkot

סֻכּוֹת

This is a sukkah. When you look through the roof of a sukkah, you can see the sky. At night you can see the stars.

A sukkah is a hut that Jews build for the holiday of Sukkot. On Sukkot it is a mitzvah to eat, drink and sleep in the sukkah.

The sukkah reminds us of things that happened a long time ago.

Sukkot in the Wilderness

The Jews were once slaves in Egypt. With God's help, they escaped. It took them forty years to walk from Egypt to the land of Israel. The Jews spent a long time in the wilderness. They spent many nights sleeping out in sukkot.

Sukkot in the Fields

When Joshua led the Jewish people into the Land of Israel they became farmers. Each family had its own fields. Every fall they went out in the fields to gather the harvest. They built sukkot to live in while they gathered their harvests.

Sukkot in Jerusalem

King Solomon was the son of King David. He built a big beautiful Temple on the top of a mountain in Jerusalem. Jews came to give thanks to God at the Temple in Jerusalem.

Three times a year, Jews left their homes and brought the best of their harvests to the Temple. Many of the Jews who came to Jerusalem spent the week-long holiday living in sukkot.

Decorate this sukkah.

Here are a lulav and an etrog.

A lulav is made up of 1 palm branch,
2 willow branches and 3 branches of myrtle.

palm

willow

myrtle

An etrog is a fruit
sort of like a lemon.

etrog

Which of these lulavim is correct?

Lulav 1   Lulav 2   Lulav 3

Today we still make Sukkot into a week-long celebration. We eat and drink in the sukkah. We even do something called *ushpizin.* We invite famous Jews from history to join us in the sukkah.

The invitation list includes Abraham, Sarah, Isaac, Rebekkah, Jacob, Rachel, Leah, Joseph, Moses, Miriam, Aaron, Hannah, David and Esther.

Shemini Atzeret

At the end of the week of Sukkot there is another holiday called *Shemini Atzeret.* It comes just before the beginning of the winter rains. It is the holiday on which we begin to ask God for rain in our daily prayers.

שִׂמְחַת תּוֹרָה

Simhat Torah

This is a Torah. Torah means "teaching." The Torah is a handwritten scroll that contains the Five Books of Moses.

The Torah teaches us stories and laws. It teaches us how to lead a good Jewish life.

Jews read part of the Torah every week. We start at the beginning and finish the whole Torah in a year. As soon as we are finished, we start all over again. On *Simhat Torah* we start over by reading the first words. For Jews, the Torah is a never-ending book.

The text showing in this Torah is from Genesis, chapter 32. It tells the story of Jacob wrestling with the angel.

Simhat Torah

A *simhah* is a happy occasion. Simhat Torah is a special occasion for the Torah. We give the Torah a party. There is singing and dancing. We wave flags. We even have a Torah parade.

On Simhat Torah we take out all of the Torah scrolls and march around the synagogue seven times.

The Torah Service

Jews read the Torah at services on Shabbat. *Aliyah* is a Hebrew word that means "going up." We say that a person makes *aliyah* when he or she moves to Israel. We also call the honor of being called to the Torah an *aliyah*, a going up.

After every Torah reading, two more people are given *aliyot* called *hagbahah* and *g'lilah*. To do *hagbahah* a person must be very strong. *Hagbahah* is sort of like weight lifting. The person who does *hagbahah* lifts the Torah high over his or her head so that everyone can see it. Torah is for every Jew. The person who does *g'lilah* helps to roll and dress the Torah.

Dress the Torah in the right order.

Number the items in the order they are put on the Torah.

Shabbat

שַׁבָּת

שבת ויום טוב

Shabbat

Shabbat is a day set aside to rest, pray, and be with our families and friends. On Shabbat, we take a break from work and school.

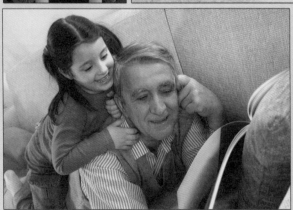

The Torah teaches us that God created the universe in six days. On the seventh day, God made Shabbat and rested. We are commanded to follow God's example. It is a mitzvah for us to work for six days and then rest on Shabbat. Shabbat is when we take a recess from our regular work and become re-created.

Shabbat is something we make. Making Shabbat takes work.

Shabbat takes preparation.

Which of these things can be used to make Shabbat?

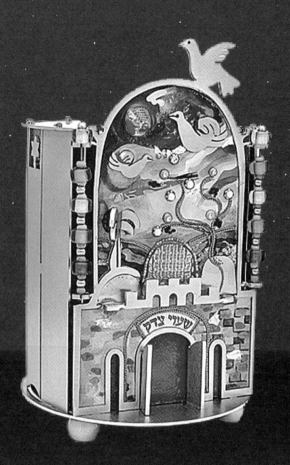

These are tzedakah boxes. Giving tzedakah is another way we prepare for Shabbat.

Tzedakah is the mitzvah of giving some of what we have to help other people who are in need. Just before Shabbat begins we put a few coins in the tzedakah box. It helps us find our Shabbat spirit.

This is a table. It is a place where we eat, talk, spend time as a family, and maybe even do homework.

This is a Shabbat table. It is an ordinary table that has been prepared for Shabbat. He we pray, talk, eat, study, sing, and become closer as a family.

Welcoming Shabbat

These are Shabbat candles. We begin Shabbat by lighting them just before the sun sets.

Shabbat is a good time to have guests. After the candles are lit, we gather around the table and sing *Shalom Aleikhem*. This Shabbat song welcomes guests. It also welcomes the Shabbat angels.

This is a Kiddush cup. It teaches us that a few words can change everything. "Kiddush" means "holy." It is the name of the *brakhah* said over a cup of wine on Shabbat and holidays. By saying a few words over a cup of wine we make Shabbat our holy time.

A *brakhah* is a blessing. A blessing is a wish. On Shabbat, parents ask God to bless their children. With a hug and with a few words they share their love as a hope for the future.

These are _hallot_.

A _hallah_ is braided bread that often comes with raisins or sesame seeds or poppy seeds. It can be round or square, big or small. It is delicious!

After the short service is finished it is finally time to eat the Shabbat dinner.

The Emperor, the Rabbi and a Spice Called Shabbat

Antoninus was a Roman Emperor. He had a good friend named Rabbi Yehudah ha-Nasi. One Shabbat, Rabbi Yehudah prepared lunch for his friend. The food was cold because the rabbi did not cook on Shabbat. Still, Antoninus pronounced everything "delicious."

"Mmmmm," said Rabbi Yehudah, raising his eyebrows like he knew a secret but couldn't tell.

Later that week the Emperor again went to the rabbi's house for dinner. This time the rabbi served him a piping hot meal. Antoninus tasted everything.

"The meat is okay," he said to the rabbi, "and the vegetables aren't bad, but I enjoyed the last meal much more. This food is missing something."

Rabbi Yehudah loved his friend and so he tried not to laugh.

"Well, something is missing," said the Emperor. "Did you forget something, or is it a secret recipe that has been handed down from one Jewish family to another year after year after year? Come on, you can tell me. What is it?"

"Okay, my friend, you're right," replied Rabbi Yehudah. "Something is missing. But you won't find it in the pantry. You won't find it in the cellar either. You won't find it in the cabinet, in the rear or on top. You won't even find it in my box of secret recipes that have been handed down from one Jewish family to another for year after year after year."

"What's missing," continued Rabbi Yehudah "is a spice that can't be grown, can't be mixed, can't be found or tasted anywhere. You see," he said, "what's really missing is not an ingredient at all, but the Shabbat itself." (Talmud Shabbat 119a)

Shabbat Day

Shabbat is a time when Jews gather in the synagogue.

In the synagogue we pray and sing. We hear the Torah being read. We spend time with our friends.

Shabbat is one time when families join together to become a community.

Ending Shabbat

When we can see at least three stars we know that it is really nighttime. We can end Shabbat any time after three stars can be counted.

Here are a Kiddush cup, a Spice box, and a *Havdalah* candle. These three things are used to end Shabbat.

Havdalah means "division."

The *havdalah* ceremony divides Shabbat from the week. It is a way of saying "good-bye" to Shabbat. It is also a way of saying "hello" to the new week.

Hanukkah

חֲנֻכָּה

What We Do on Hanukkah

This is a *hanukkiyah*. It is also called a Hanukkah menorah. It holds the lights of Hanukkah.

Hanukkah lasts for eight days. On the first night we light one candle on our *hanukkiyah*. We light two candles on the second night. Every night we add another candle.

When we light the *hanukkiyah* we become part of the story of Hanukkah.

Circle all the *hanukkiyot*.

48

Hanukkah means "dedication." There is a dedication when a new building or bridge is opened for the first time.

Every year on Hanukkah we remember when the Maccabees rededicated the Temple in Jerusalem. The Temple in Jerusalem was turned into a place where Greek idols were worshipped. The Maccabees fought back. They won a war and cleaned up the Temple. The Maccabees threw out all the Greek idols. Then they lit the Great Menorah.

This is a dreidle. In Hebrew it is called a *sevivon*. The dreidle has four sides. Each side has a Hebrew letter. We use the dreidle to play a game.

When you spin the dreidle and it lands on נ *Nun*, you get *nichts*, nothing.

When you spin the dreidle and it lands on ג *Gimmel*, you get *ganz*, everything.

When you spin the dreidle and it lands on ה *Hey*, you get *halb*, half.

When you spin the dreidle and it lands on ש *Shin*, you have to *shtel*, put in.

ג Gimmel means you win. Circle the dreidles that have a ג Gimmel.

The *sevivon* teaches an important lesson.

The four Hebrew letters נ *Nun*, ג *Gimmel*, ה *Hey*, and שׁ *Shin* stand for four Hebrew words.

נֵס גָּדוֹל הָיָה שָׁם

Nes Gadol Hayah Sham.

A great miracle happened there.

The story of Ḥanukkah is the story of a miracle. It is the story of finding light when everything seems to be dark.

The Story of <u>H</u>anukkah

The story of <u>H</u>anukkah is the story of a miracle.

Antiochus was a wicked king who wanted everyone in his kingdom to be exactly the same. He tried to make all the Jews be just like everyone else. He ordered them to bow down and pray to idols. Some Jews said, "No."

Antiochus had a big and powerful army. No one thought that just a few Jews could beat them.

Mattathias was a Jew who would not bow down to idols He fought back. He told the other Jews, "Let everyone who believes in following the Torah follow me." They hid in the mountains and sneaked down to fight Antiochus' army.

The Jews who fought back became the Maccabbees. After years of fighting they won the war. They were free to live as Jews. They didn't have to be like everyone else.

They came to the Temple and found that it was a mess. The Maccabees cleaned up the Temple. When it was ready they held a special service. They lit the Great Menorah and celebrated for eight days.

Hanukkah is still eight of the happiest days in the Jewish year.

Hanukkah is a fun holiday. It is a time for games and parties. We give gifts and eat potato latkes and *sufganiyot* (jelly donuts). Latkes and *sufganiyot* are cooked in oil. Oil reminds us of the oil the Maccabees used to relight the Great Menorah. On Hanukkah we are proud to be Jews.

Feeling Jewish

The Maccabees were Jews who believed that Jews should do Jewish things. They were proud to be Jews. Sometimes we want to be like the Maccabees.

When was one time you were really proud to be a Jew?

_____

_____

54

Rules for lighting a Hanukkiyah

A. Always put the candles in beginning on the right side of the hanukkiyah.

B. The *shamash* should always be the highest light. Light it first then say all the blessings.

C. Always light the new candle first each night. Then light the candles starting on the left.

SECOND NIGHT

FIRST NIGHT

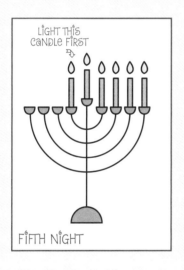

FIFTH NIGHT

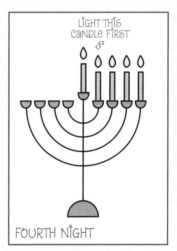

FOURTH NIGHT

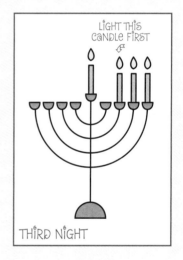

THIRD NIGHT

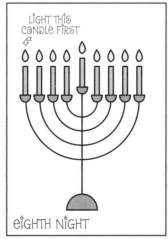

EIGHTH NIGHT

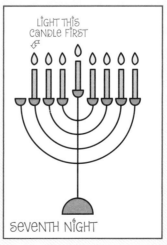

SEVENTH NIGHT

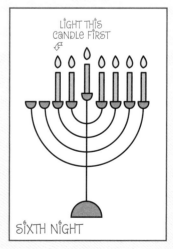

SIXTH NIGHT

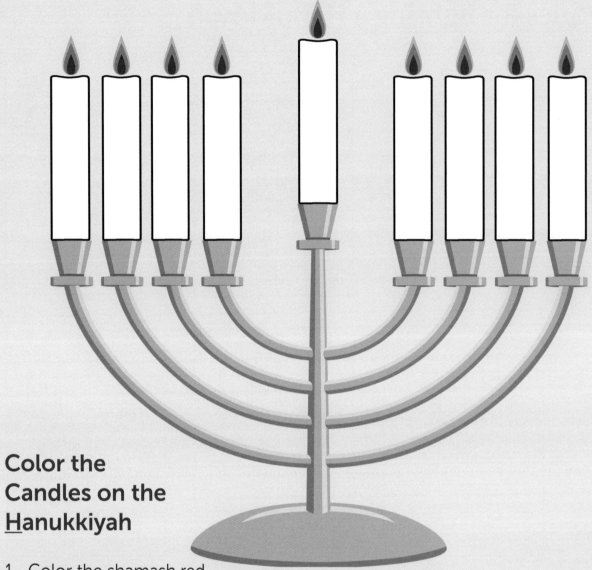

Color the Candles on the Hanukkiyah

1. Color the shamash red.
2. Color the candle lit first on the first night blue.
3. Color the candle lit first on the second night green.
4. Color the candle lit first on the third night pink.
5. Color the candle lit first on the fourth night purple.
6. Color the candle lit first on the fifth night orange.
7. Color the candle lit first on the sixth night brown.
8. Color the candle lit first on the seventh night light blue.
9. Leave the candle lit first on the eighth night white.

ט"ו בִּשְׁבַט

Tu B'Shvat

57

Jews have a birthday for trees. This is because of a law in the Torah that says, "No eating fruit from a tree's first five years." (Leviticus 19:23-25)

How do you know how old a tree is? The Rabbis figured out a trick. They decided that Tu B'Shvat was every tree's birthday. On Tu B'Shvat every new tree is one year older. When a tree is five years old, we can eat its fruit.

Tu B'Shvat is the fifteenth day of the Hebrew month of *Shvat*. Tu B'Shvat is every tree's birthday.

Activity: Tu B'Shvat

Today is Tu B'Shvat. Circle in red the tree with ribbons on them. They are two-year-old trees. Circle in blue the trees with fruit and no ribbons. They are one-year-old trees. The trees with no fruit will be one year old next year.

Planting Trees

It is a Tu b'Shvat tradition to plant trees. Sometimes it is paying for trees that will be planted in Israel. Sometimes it is planting trees in our own neighbor or yard.

Trees help the world. Some of them give us food. Some provide shade. Trees also keep the air clean.

Celebrating Trees

Tu b'Shvat is a time to celebrate trees. In Israel students often go into the forest and dance around trees. It is a time to remember how trees are important. This is a holiday where we learn more about how trees help us. It is a "green" Jewish holiday.

Purim

פּוּרִים

Things We Do On Purim

This is a *gragger*. In Hebrew it is called a *ra'ashan*. No matter which name you use it still makes lots of noise. The gragger teaches us one of the Purim's great lessons. When we work together, we are stronger than evil.

This is the *megillah*. It is the scroll that tells the story of Queen Esther. Like a *Sefer Torah* (Torah scroll), the megillah must be written by hand.

Esther was a Jewish woman who became the Queen of Persia. She saved the Jewish people from a wicked man named Haman. Haman wanted to kill every single Jew.

These are *hamantashen*. They are special Purim cookies that are named after Haman. Hamantashen are shaped like triangles. No one is sure why. Some people think that Haman wore a three-cornered hat. Other people think that Haman had big ears that were shaped like triangles.

 When we read the story of Esther from the megillah, We make lots of noise every time Haman's name is read. We spin our  graggers. We shout and stomp our feet. We make sure that no one can hear the evil name Haman. Together we can make lots of noise. Together we are very strong.

Purim is a time for parties. Purim is costumes and carnivals. It is graggers and hamantashen. Purim is reading the megillah, acting silly, shouting and making noise, winning prizes, giving gifts, and having the best time.

The Story of Esther

Ahasuerus was the King. He gave a party for all the important men. Queen Vashti gave a party for all the important women. King Ahasuerus asked Vashti to come to visit his party. She told him "NO!"

The king decided that he would choose a new queen. He sent out a command that all the beautiful women in the kingdom must come to the palace.

Esther was a very beautiful Jewish woman. She had no parents. Her uncle Mordechai took care of her. Before she came to the palace, her uncle told her, "Do not tell anyone that you are a Jew." Ahasuerus chose Esther to be his new queen.

One day Mordechai heard two men planning to kill the king. He told the king's guards. Ahasuerus' life was saved!

Haman was the king's chief advisor. The king made it a rule that everyone must bow down to Haman. Jews don't bow down to humans. Mordechai wouldn't bow down to Haman. Haman was angry. He hated Mordechai. He hated all Jews. He asked the king to let him kill all the Jews.

Haman pulled *Purim* out of a hat to pick a date to get even. Purim are "lots." It became a royal command that all Jews would be killed on the 13th day of the month of Adar.

Mordechai went to see Esther. He told her that she must go to the king and save the Jewish people.

66

Esther went to see the king. He was glad to see her. She asked him to come to a party and to bring Haman. He said "Yes."

One night the king couldn't sleep. He had his servants read to him. They read from the book of court records. The king learned that Mordechai had once saved his life but had received no reward.

The king sent for Haman. He asked him, "How should I honor a person?" Haman told his idea. The king then said, "Do all this for Mordechai."

Haman and the king came to Esther's party. Esther told the king, "Someone wants to kill me and all my people." He asked, "Who?" She said, "Haman." The king got rid of Haman and made Mordechai his chief advisor.

Everything was okay.

What We Learn From Purim

Esther was just one Jew, but she saved the whole Jewish people. Her story teaches us that every person can be a hero. Every Jew is important. On Purim we remember the story of Esther. To make sure that we never forget that every Jew can be like Esther, we make sure that the day on which we tell her story is a day filled with fun.

How We Remember the Story

Match the Purim custom with the idea it helps us remember.

 Haman, the bad guy

 The Megillah

 Esther, the Hero

 The Gragger

 Haman was defeated

 Hamantashen

The Two Gifts

Ever since the first Purim, Jews have sent special gifts to their friends and families called *shela<u>h</u> manot*. *Shela<u>h</u> manot* is sending small gifts of food.

There is a second kind of gift we give on Purim. Mordechai ordered Jews to perform the mitzvah of giving *mattanot le-evyonim*, gifts to the poor.

Help Amy Deliver *Shela<u>h</u> Manot*

Amy's mother asked her to take the family's *shela<u>h</u> manot* to five houses. She has to visit:

- Uncle Asher
- The Kaplans
- Mrs. Rowe, her teacher
- Amy's best friend Susan
- Grandma Esther

Draw the way for Amy to make this trip.

Purim is the happiest day in the Jewish year. We do fun things like go to carnivals, dress in costumes, have a special Purim dinner. Being happy on Purim is a mitzvah. We remember the heroes, Mordechai and Esther, who saved the whole Jewish people. We remember that every Jew can be a hero.

Who is your Jewish hero? _____

_____

פֶּסַח

Passover

This is What We Do on Passover

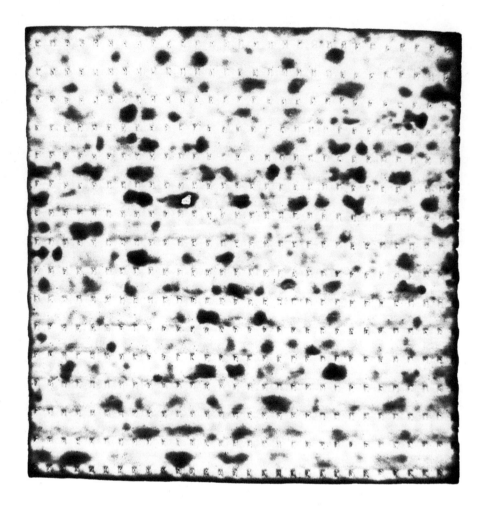

This is a piece of *matzah*. Matzah is the special flat bread we eat on *Pesah*. Pesah is the Hebrew name for Passover.

When our families were slaves we had to leave in a hurry. We didn't have time to knead bread and wait for it to rise. Instead we just mixed flour and water and baked it into matzah.

On Pesah it is a mitzvah to eat matzah. When we eat it we remember what is was like when we were slaves in Egypt. We remember the pain of slavery. We make sure that other people will not suffer in the way that we did.

Help Israel make it from slavery to freedom.

This book is a *Haggadah*. Haggadah means "the telling." On Pesa<u>h</u> it is a mitzvah to tell the story of how God brought all the Jewish families who were slaves in Egypt to freedom in the land of Israel. We read the story of Pesa<u>h</u> from the Haggadah.

This table is all set up for a *Seder*. Seder means "order." It is the special service we have in our homes on the first night of Pesa<u>h</u>. On the table you can see candles and Kiddush cups. There is a cup for Elijah and wine. There are also matzah and the Seder plate.

At the Seder our table becomes a place of prayer and a place of study. It is also a place to eat wonderful food.

Look at this Seder plate. On it you can see:

Z'ro'a, a roasted shank bone.

Betzah, an egg.

Maror, the bitter herb.

<u>H</u>*aroset*, a special mixture of nuts and fruit.

Karpas, a fresh vegetable.

Each of these foods teaches a lesson. Each of these things help us remember another part of the Pesa<u>h</u> story.

The very first Seder took place on the night before our families left Egypt. It was a scary night. No one was sure if God could really lead us to freedom. Each family took a lamb and prepared it for dinner. On their last night in Egypt, our families ate the lamb as a Pesah offering. They ate it along with *matzah* and *maror*.

The Seder

The *Karpas* (Fresh Vegetable) reminds us of spring. Pesa<u>h</u> comes in the spring. We dip the karpas in salt water. Salt water reminds us of the tears of slavery.

The *Betzah* (the egg) also reminds us of spring.

The *Maror* (the bitter herbs) reminds us of |the bitterness of slavery. We eat it with *Matzah* the way they did in Egypt.

Matzah is also called the "bread of freedom." First we had bitterness. Now we have freedom.

The *<u>H</u>aroset* reminds us of the cement we used in Egypt. We were forced to build cities for Pharaoh.

The *Z'ro'a* reminds us of the lamb we ate on the last night in Egypt.

At the seder we drink four glasses of grape juice or wine. In the Torah God makes four promises to the Jewish people.

"**I will bring you out.**"

"**I will deliver you.**"

"**I will redeem you.**"

And "**I take you as my people**" (Exodus 6:6-7). The four glasses remind us of the four promises.

We have Pesa<u>h</u> because these promises all came true.

During the Seder we hide the Afikomen. Three matzot (unleaven bread) are used during the Seder. The middle matzah is broken in half. Half of it is hidden. After dinner all the children go hunting for the afikomen. There is a prize for finding it. The parents know it is the right matzah because they match the half that is hidden to the half they have kept.

Find the afikomen in the picture below.

The foods and glasses of juice tell the Seder's story.

We were slaves in Egypt. We cried out to God. God heard us. God made ten plagues happen. Pharoah let us go. We left Egypt and went into freedom. God made a miracle and made the Reed Sea divide. We were now safe. Our family sang and danced and thanked God.

At the seder we act out the story of leaving Egypt.

Passover Crossword Puzzle

Fill in the missing letters on this crossword puzzle.

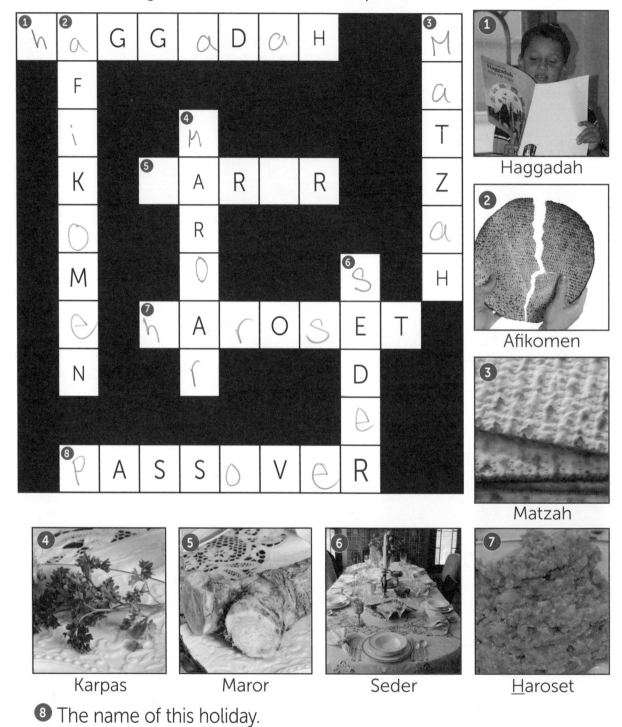

Haggadah

Afikomen

Matzah

Karpas

Maror

Seder

<u>H</u>aroset

8 The name of this holiday.

Yom ha-Atzmaút

יוֹם הָעַצְמָאוּת

Israel's Birthday

Nations have birthdays. The birthday of the United States is the 4th of July. It is called "Independence Day." Israel's birthday is called "*Yom ha-Atzma'ut.*" This is Hebrew for "Independence Day." It happens on the 5th of the Jewish month of Iyar. It is usually in May.

Israelis dance in the streets on Yom ha-Atzma'ut. There are parades and celebrations. It is a day of parties. Many Israelis make a picnic or a barbecue. Israel flags are flying everywhere. There are fireworks at night.

Tel Aviv

Jews all over the world celebrate Yom ha-Atzma'ut, too. There are parties and parades in many cities. There are even special prayers that are said. Often Jews eat Israel food as part of the celebration. Jews everywhere know that Israel is also their home.

The Israeli Flag

The Israeli flag has two blue stripes like on a tallit. The tallit is a prayer shawl worn at daytime services.

Color the two stripes blue.

The Israeli flag also has a blue Jewish Star. In Hebrew the star is called a Magen David. This means "The Shield of David." A six-pointed star helped to protect King David.

Color the Magen David blue, too.

Hatikvah

The national anthem of the United States is "The Star Spangled Banner." The national anthem of Canada is "Oh Canada." The national anthem of Israel is called "*Hatikvah.*" *Hatikvah* mean "the hope." Jews stand when Hatikvah is sung. When we hear it we are connected to the State of Israel and Jews all over the world.

This menorah is also a symbol of Israel.

Finding *Ima*

Elana has gotten lost in all the celebration. She is on one side of the street. Her mother is on the other. Draw a line that leads Elana through the dancing and helps her get back to her mother.

Shavuot

שָׁבוּעוֹת

Shavuot

Hag ha-Shavuot means "The Festival of Weeks". The Torah tells us that it took forty-nine days for our family to travel from Egypt to the foot of Mount Sinai. Jews count forty-nine days after Pesa<u>h</u>. The fiftieth day is *Shavuot*. Shavuot means "weeks." Shavuot is seven weeks after Pesa<u>h</u>.

Z'man Matan Torah means "The Time of the Gift of Torah." Shavuot is the day when we stood at Mount Sinai and God gave us the Torah. All of Israel gathered at the foot of the mountain. God spoke to us from the mountain top. Israel said, "We will obey the Torah and we will listen to it." (Exodus 24:7)

Trace the letters to complete the Ten Commandments,

Things We Do on Shavuot

Study Torah All Night

Remember, Jewish days begin at night. We start a Jewish holiday by lighting candles. It is a tradition to stay up and study Torah at the beginning of Shavuot.

Eating Milk Products

It is a custom to eat milk products and not meat on Shavuot. Fifteen times in the Torah we are told that God will bring us to a "land of milk and honey." Israel is that land. On Shavuot we eat milk because of that promise.

Draw an "X" through the foods we do not eat on Shavuot.

Decorating Homes and Synagogues with Plants and Flowers

When we were at Mount Sinai, it was blooming and full of greenery and flowers. Mount Sinai is in the middle of the wilderness. These plants and flowers remind us that Shavuot was the time for the harvest.

94

Reading the Book of Ruth

The book of Ruth is a love story. It shows the love of a woman for her friend. It also tells the story of a great love between a man and woman. We read this story because it is a story about harvests. And we read this story because it shows how someone can convert to Judaism and accept the Torah.

This is the same thing that all of Israel did at Mount Sinai.

Confirmation

At Mount Sinai we said "WE WILL OBEY THE TORAH AND WE WILL LISTEN TO IT (Exodus 24:7)." At Confirmation ninth or tenth graders say the same thing. Confirmation is a ceremony that happens on Shavuot. It is a time when students finish their formal Jewish education. They say that they are committed to live a Jewish life.